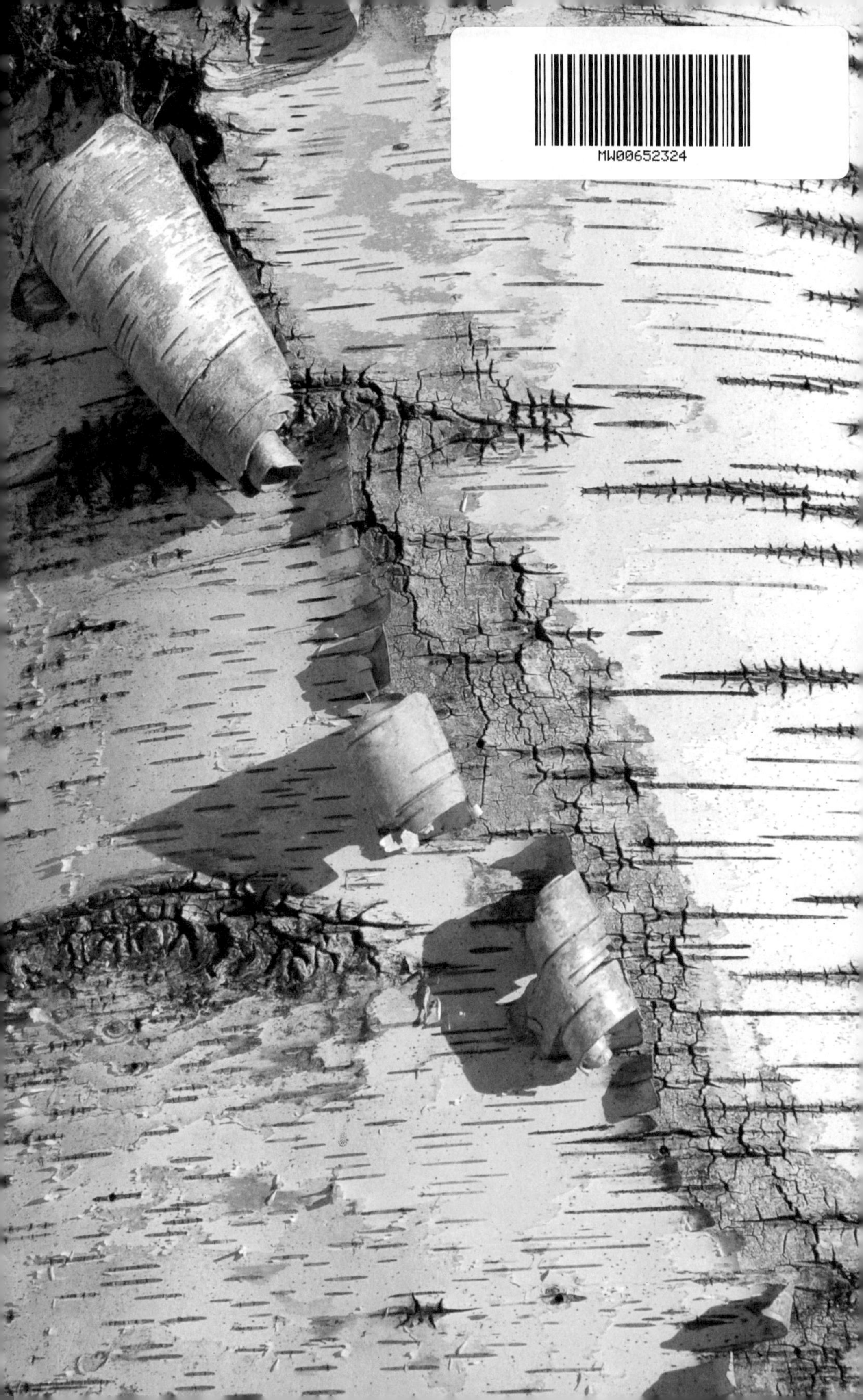
MW00652324

PADDLING THROUGH TIME

The Northern Forest Canoe Trail
is a 740-mile heritage water trail
through the Northern Forest Region:
New York, Vermont, Québec,
New Hampshire, and Maine.

PADDLING THROUGH TIME

The Story of the Northern Forest Canoe Trail

ACKNOWLEDGEMENTS:

This book is the result of numerous contributors: writers, photographers, editors, and reviewers. As such, it embodies the Northern Forest Canoe Trail's commitment to celebrating the many voices and stories flowing in this water route. We publish *Paddling Through Time* with gratitude to the many minds, hearts, and hands that have shaped it.

Special thanks to Patrick Jennings, M.A., University of Oklahoma, 1994, for his research and original paper, and to Mike Wilson and Jennifer Waite who devoted countless hours to write this story, with the assistance of Dean Bennett and Gilbert Center.

We also thank Hallie Bond and Jane Beck for their thoughtful contributions, and Donna and John Moody, and Fred Wiseman for their wisdom and insights. Thanks also to the many contributors of photography and images, and especially to Clyde Smith for his photographic advice.

The Northern Forest Canoe Trail extends special thanks to Lois McClure and The Timberland Company, whose support enabled us to bring this book to fruition.

Kate Williams
Executive Director, Northern Forest Canoe Trail
Summer 2006

ISBN: 0-9786697-0-3

The Northern Forest Canoe Trail produced this book, with technical assistance from the National Park Service's Rivers and Trails Conservation Assistance Program. The National Park Service's Challenge Cost Share Program supported this project. Points of view are those of the authors, and do not represent the Department of the Interior's position.

Book design: The Laughing Bear Associates, Montpelier, Vermont
Technical support: David Goodman; Printing: Villanti & Sons, Printers, Milton, Vermont

For more information, please contact:

NORTHERN FOREST CANOE TRAIL

P.O. Box 565, Waitsfield, Vermont 05673; 802.496.2285 (tel); 802.496.2785 (fax)

info@NorthernForestCanoeTrail.org

CONTENTS

Preface 9

The Story of the Northern Forest Canoe Trail 15

The Route of the Northern Forest Canoe Trail 16

Waterways & the First Peoples 19

Newcomers: Conflict & Change 29

Rivers for Settlement & Industry 35

Recreation, Renewal & Conservation 43

The Northern Forest Canoe Trail Today 49

Afterword 52

The Northern Forest Canoe Trail Organization 54

Resources, Notes & Artwork Credits 57

"The Northern Forest Canoe Trail is a heritage trail—as close as we can come to a time machine. Paddlers jump from the present through many pasts as they slide from wild to rural to urban and back along a thousand-year-old water highway."

– Ron Canter
Adirondack Life
2002

PREFACE

Water, humans, boats. Since the earliest days of civilization, these three elements have shaped the ways people live, work, and trade around the world. The Northern Forest Canoe Trail invites you to explore the historical and cultural ways these three elements link what is now the international border region of New York, Vermont, Québec, New Hampshire, and Maine.

The Northern Forest, the largest intact ecosystem east of the Mississippi River, comprises some 30 million acres of northern Maine, New Hampshire, Vermont, and New York, and blends into adjacent Canada. Boreal and northern hardwood forests blanket rolling hills and rugged mountains. This rich panoply of streams, rivers, lakes, ponds, and wetlands helps form the headwaters of all the major river systems in the northeastern United States.

Hudson. Connecticut. Androscoggin. Kennebec. Penobscot. Allagash. These names identify just some of the mighty rivers emerging from the Northern Forest. Like modern north-south interstates, these big rivers flow from the region's heart. Like back roads, meanwhile, their tributaries connect the region from east to west, providing access to magical and remote places.

While our travel on these waterways today is primarily for recreation, not so long ago the rivers, lakes, and streams of the Northern Forest played a vital role in people's daily lives.

Until the automobile age, just about anything people did in the Northern Forest, they did in boats. They waged war, filled the larder, visited their neighbors, went to work, proposed marriage, filled blast furnaces and charcoal kilns, and harvested lumber. Boats have been used for leisure as well as for business; over the past century and a half, the Northern Forest has been the nation's center of inland pleasure boating. Both the city folk and the people who live here have hunted, fished, painted, photographed, and generally refreshed their souls from a boat.

Some large bodies of water in the region have floated ships — the American navy was born on Lake Champlain — but the brooks, streams, and small rivers of the Northern Forest are best traveled in small boats. The many cultures that have used these waterways left a rich tradition of canoes and rowing craft. The Algonkian peoples gave us the canoe, the form that has been the most enduring. European settlers brought with them the idea of the rowboat. Some boat types from other cultures are now at home here, as well. Nineteenth-century paddlers introduced a wooden version of the Inuit-style kayak, and their descendants take brightly-colored synthetics down every trickle they can find.

You are part of a long tradition as you paddle through time on the Northern Forest Canoe Trail.

Thanks to the combination of passable waterways and boats to navigate them, a rich culture has evolved in the Northern Forest, one that reflects the struggles and triumphs of people building lives for themselves in a remote forest region. The stories to be found along the Northern Forest Canoe Trail offer rare glimpses into the ever-changing relationships within the Northern Forest landscape.

Until the automobile age, just about anything people did in the Northern Forest, they did in boats. They waged war, filled the larder, visited their neighbors, went to work, proposed marriage, filled blast furnaces and charcoal kilns, and harvested lumber.

While the rivers, streams, and lakes of the canoe trail link the Northern Forest region, it is the people who bridge differences and bring understanding through their stories and traditions. The Native Americans whose ancestors first explored these routes tell countless stories drawing on centuries of intimate relationships with the landscape. Other stories tell of the logging camp cook in Saranac Lake who used to bake bread twice a day, make 27 pies, use a whole case of eggs for breakfast and cut up a half a pig and half a beef every other day; of bootlegging and smuggling escapades in towns along the Canadian border; of the hardy river driver dynamiting a log jam on the Androscoggin River.

Even place names along the canoe trail help peel back the layers of history. We have the Missisquoi River which is Abenaki for "crooked river" or "river which doubles back on itself," and

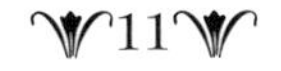

The Northern Forest At-A-Glance

The Northern Forest Canoe Trail traverses 22 rivers and streams, 56 lakes and ponds, and more than a dozen watersheds as it passes through the area known as the Northern Forest. In this boreal landscape, the rivers and forests have always been the center of ecology, culture, and economics. Names like Missisquoi and Ammonoosuc recall the first people to ply the waters in birchbark canoes, hunting and trading along the same routes that eventually brought European explorers inland. Water power fueled growing communities and industries. Rivers carried logs from forest to mill for lumber to build the growing cities of the Northeast. City-dwellers followed waterways into the wilderness for rejuvenation and sport. Today, for both recreation and livelihood, rivers and forests continue to be central to life here, and the Trail flows like a common thread, weaving together the historical, cultural, and natural stories of the region.

THE NORTHERN FOREST:

- 30 million acres: the largest area of intact forest east of the Mississippi
- 1.5 million residents
- Includes the headwaters of the major rivers of the northeastern U.S.: Hudson, Connecticut, Androscoggin, Kennebec, Penobscot, St. John
- Significantly reforested since the 1850s when region was the leading timber producer in the world

Lake Memphremagog which means "wide water" or "at the big waters." These and other place names tell the stories of people who read the landscape like a map, using names to help navigate routes known only through experience and oral tradition.

As little as 50 years ago, there were places in the Northern Forest where people grew up with no electricity, no telephone or modern conveniences, and few roads—living off the land, utilizing wild roots and herbs, fish and game, and their gardens.

While the rivers, streams, and lakes of the canoe trail link the Northern Forest region, it is the people who bridge differences and bring understanding through their stories and traditions.

Today this way of life seems like ancient history. Still, most of this region's residents, Native Americans and newcomers alike, share an interest in the stories of the people who lived here before us—tales of ingenuity, struggle, craftsmanship, heritage, poverty, and success. The stories you'll find along the Northern Forest Canoe Trail offer a simple and resounding affirmation: traditions change, yet they still abound, tying those of the Northern Forest to their heritage and to each other.

As you set off on your own explorations of the Northern Forest Canoe Trail, feel the water's currents carrying you through time and place, appreciate the grace with which your boat floats down a wild river, and listen for the stories of people along the way. Water, humans, and boats—the story of the Northern Forest Canoe Trail.

– Jane Beck
Executive Director, The Vermont Folklife Center

– Hallie Bond
Curator, Adirondack Museum

– Mike Wilson
Senior Program Director, Northern Forest Center

"Indeed, what makes the Northern Forest Canoe Trail such a classic journey is that it cuts a clean cross-section right through the heart of the region's natural and cultural treasures, reconnecting us with the earth and with the past."

– Stephen Gorman
Northeastern Wilds: Journeys of Discovery in the Northern Forest
2002

THE STORY OF THE NORTHERN FOREST CANOE TRAIL

Stretching 740 miles from Old Forge, New York, to Fort Kent, Maine, the Northern Forest Canoe Trail is a chain of rivers, streams, lakes, and portages that for centuries allowed people to explore, travel, trade, and build communities. It is a route that traverses the largest tract of forestland in the northeastern United States, guiding travelers through whitewater gorges, quiet marshes, and wide lakes; carrying them through deep forests, working farm and timber landscapes, and village centers. Today this trail offers a remarkable journey by canoe or kayak where one experiences the region's rich history.

This book traces the story behind the Trail.

THE ROUTE OF THE
NORTHERN FOREST
CANOE TRAIL
117
40
133
Mansonville
55
Newport
91
89
Plattsburgh
3
Saranac
Lake
Burlington
Morrisville
Tupper
Lake
Lake Placid
3
Adirondack
Mountains
Old Forge
30
4
Leban

CANADA
UNITED STATES
Fort Kent
Allagash
Clayton Lake
Chesuncook
Millinocket
Jackman
Greenville
West Forks
Stratton
Rangeley
Errol
North Stratford
Lancaster
Mount Washington
Bangor
Portland
NEW HAMPSHIRE
MAINE
Atlantic Ocean
175
138
20
11
161
163
95
2
201
3
26
302
495

"The ancient canoe routes fall into four general categories: major routes along the great north-south rivers; short routes over interconnecting tributaries for travel between watersheds; cut-offs for safety and convenience; and neighborhood routes that were byways through hunting and trapping regions, but had poor connections to any other place."

– David Cook
Above the Gravel Bar:
The Indian Canoe Routes of Maine
1985

WATERWAYS & THE FIRST PEOPLES

The end of the last Ice Age 12,000 to 13,000 years ago revealed a Northern Forest landscape much different from the one we see today. As the glaciers retreated northward, they left behind a mountainous but barren and watery landscape that gradually evolved from open tundra to the thickly forested landscape we now know. Into this new land came the ancestors of the eastern Native American peoples; Native American oral tradition holds that the Wabanaki people were created in this place. Archeologists agree that there is clear evidence of Native American peoples in the northeast back to 12,000 years ago. As the landscape evolved over time into a dense forest environment, so did these peoples' ways of life.

Trade between tribes and communities proved an important part of indigenous life in the Northern Forest—as was periodic warfare and raiding. West of Lake Champlain, the Five Nations of the Iroquois, the Haudenosaunee Confederation, controlled most of the water routes through the Adirondacks and west to the Great Lakes.

Between Lake Champlain and the Atlantic Ocean lived the many tribes of the Wabanaki, "people of the dawn," including the Abenaki, Malicite (or Maliseet), Micmac, Penobscot, and Passamaquoddy. Those living in coastal areas, such as the Passamaquoddy, had access to valuable ocean resources such as fish and salt. The Penobscots controlled Maine's Moosehead Lake, an important source of rhyolite—a volcanic rock much like flint that proved essential in toolmaking. Other tribes guarded concentrations of other resources, or controlled travel routes vital to trade and transportation. East-west travel proved difficult, though, as the region's rugged topography and thick forests made travel along footpaths slow and energy intensive, since a single person could carry only a limited amount of goods.

Rivers and streams could serve as a better kind of path—water trails that could carry them through thick forests faster and more efficiently than travel on foot.

With time, the region's denizens learned that the rivers and streams could serve as a better kind of path—water trails that could carry them through thick forests faster and more efficiently than travel on foot. So, during the course of thousands of years, the Native American people of the Northern Forest, as in other areas, developed the method of water transport we now call the canoe. These vessels included birch bark, elm bark, and cedar canoes, as well as early "dugout" designs, in which a fire was set in a log, and chiseling tools such as stone adzes and gouges were used to hollow out its center.

The birch bark and other canoes and dugouts of the northeastern Native American peoples probably share the same ancient origins. Dugout canoes dated to 8,000 years old have been found in the Americas, and the strong oral history of canoeing among Native American people in the northeast suggests an ancient time depth for both the dugout and bark canoes. The river systems, including

Ice One-Mile Thick

Between 35,000 and 15,000 years ago, a vast glacier more than one mile thick known as the Laurentide Ice Sheet gouged its way southward across what is now Québec, Maine, New Hampshire, Vermont, and New York. Subsequent climatic warming caused this ice sheet to begin to recede northwards. Huge blocks of ice split off and gradually melted, creating rivers and enormous lakes. For a time, when the St. Lawrence waterway flooded in from the north, the Champlain Valley of Vermont and New York even hosted saltwater species such as whales and seals. Mountains rising above the lakes include today's northern Appalachians, Greens, and Adirondacks, a series of ranges passable in only two places at water level where the glacier tore gaps in the mountains – the north-south corridor of Lake Champlain and the Hudson River, and the east-west corridor of the Mohawk River. These wide water corridors ultimately became the warpaths of empires, and major highways connecting people, resources, and land. Tracing outward from these valleys and up into the mountains were the rivers and streams that fed the mighty waterways; together, these smaller tributaries, linked with overland paths, became the route of the Northern Forest Canoe Trail.

the east-west corridors, served as the primary conduits of both daily life and of extensive regional and continental trade, dating back many thousands of years. Even today, the Wabanaki are known as skilled travelers. Their broad knowledge of geography and travel routes guided many early non-native settlers to their new homes in this ancient land. And the Wabanaki and their northern relations in modern day Canada have continued to use these old water routes down to the present day.

The development of the canoe, and the gradual discovery of the many water trails that connected the interior lands, altered the patterns of interaction among the region's Native American inhabitants. The increase in trade, accompanied by agricultural development and population growth, quickly led to greater contact between once-isolated communities. Discovery of canoe and water trails forged new connections between peoples who had been separated by mountain ranges and distances too great to carry goods and supplies. Out of these connections, the Northern Forest Canoe Trail was born.

Small Boat

"The use of the name 'canoe' for bark watercraft does not appear to be taken from a North American Indian usage. The early French explorers and travelers called these craft 'canau'...As this also meant 'canal', the name 'canot' was soon substituted. But some early writers preferred to call the canoe 'ecorse de bouleau', or 'birchbark' and sometimes the name used was merely the generic 'petit embarkation', or small boat. The early English term was 'canoa', later 'canoe'..."

– Edwin Tappan Adney and Howard I. Chapelle,
The Bark Canoes and Skin Boats of North America,
1964

The Birchbark Canoe

Building a birchbark canoe (a *wigwaol* in the Abenaki tongue) involved crafting a light frame of trees lashed with roots or grass, covering it with tree bark, and sealing the seams with spruce gum, bear grease, and other substances. Ideally, the bark covering consisted of a single piece stripped from a large tree and turned inside out to improve water resistance. As use of the birchbark canoe spread through the region, different groups developed somewhat different designs and systems for building their canoes.

A typical 15-foot birchbark canoe weighed roughly 60 pounds, comparable to modern aluminum or plastic canoes. One person could pick up a canoe and carry it over long portages by holding it upside down on the shoulders. One canoe could transport an entire family, including several children, plus all of their packed goods and even their dogs. The Penobscot Indians called their birchbark canoes *agwiden*, which means "float lightly."

Father Rasle, a 17th century missionary living with the Abenaki people, wrote in a letter to his brother, "The canoes...are made of a single piece of bark, but the largest of them can hold six or seven persons. It is with these canoes...which has scarcely more the thickness of a crown piece, that they pass arms of the sea, and navigate the most dangerous rivers and lakes of four and five hundred leagues in circuit. I have made many voyages in this way without having run any risk."

Abenaki Village Sites

Several major bands of Abenaki lived in Vermont, each associated with a large village on a canoeable stream. The Abenakis favored village sites on bluffs on the south or west facing side of a stream. From there the surrounding countryside could be watched, with a particular eye to the west, where Lake Champlain formed an international boundary between the Abenaki lands and lands of the Iroquois / Haudenosaunee Confederacy. A bluff location also took advantage of the prevailing west winds and kept summer insects bearable. Early Europeans referred to these villages as "castles," owing to their high location and the vertically set log palisades surrounding them. During the summer months these villages swelled to their greatest size — the Missisquoi village and other Abenaki villages routinely contained 1,000-5,000 people. In late Fall, though, everyone except the old and infirm left the village and fanned out to upland family hunting territories of 20 to 100 square miles per family band. Their central feature — a stream or river and its associated watershed — clearly defined these territories.

A Sampling of Native American Place Names

Wabanaki ancestors came into the Northeast about 12,000 years ago, following the herds of caribou over post-Ice Age tundra. Many rivers and other landmarks along the canoe trail retain their Native American place names.

Modern Name	Abenaki Name	Approximate English Meaning
Maine		
Moosehead Lake	Mozôdebinebeseki	Moose Head Lake
New Hampshire		
Lake Umbagog	Wôbagok	Clear Lake
Androscoggin River	Laesikontegw	Rock Shelter River
Connecticut River	Kwenitegok	Long River
Vermont		
Lake Champlain	Bitawbagok	Lake Between
Grand Isle	Ktsimenahan	Great Island
Highgate Springs	Nebizônnibik	Medicine Water
Island Pond	Menahanbagok	Island Lake
Isle La Motte	Azibijizikok	Sheep Dung Place
Maquam Bay	Tamakwa	Beaver On Its Lodge Bay
Lake Memphremagog	Mamhlawbagok	Wide Water
Missisquoi Bay	Masipskiwibi	Flint Water
Missisquoi River	Wazowategok	Crooked River
Nulhegan River	Klahigantegok	Wooden Trap River
Swanton	Mazipskoik	Flint Place
New York		
Adirondack Mountains	Wawobadenik	White Mountains
Saranac River	Salôntegok	Sumac River

- reference: Fred Wiseman, *Voice of the Dawn*, University Press of New England, 2001 and Gordon Day, *Western Abenaki Dictionary*, Museum of Civilization, Ottawa, Ontario, 1995.

From Other Sources

Maine		
Chamberlain Lake	Apmoojenegamook	Cross Lake
Churchill Lake	Allagaskwigamook	Bark Cabin Lake

- reference: Dean Bennett, *The Wilderness From Chamberlain Farm*, Island Press/Shearwater Books, 2001.

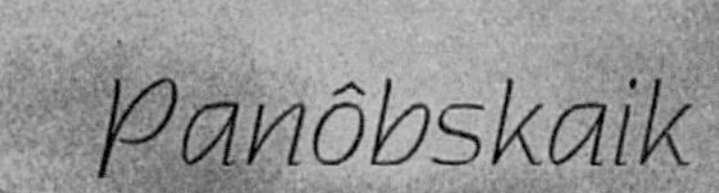
Panôbskaik
Kenebec
Molojoak
Laesik
Mozôdebinebesek
Amescanti
Narakamik
Wôbagok
Laesikantegw
Goategok
Mamhlawbagok
Menahanbagok
Pasomkasik
Ômamosek
+Mozeodebe Wadjo
+Dowabodi
Wazowategok
Wintegok
Bitawbagwizibok
Mazipskoik
Mskitegwa
Ktsimenahan
Winoskik

WOBANAKIK

Land of the Dawn

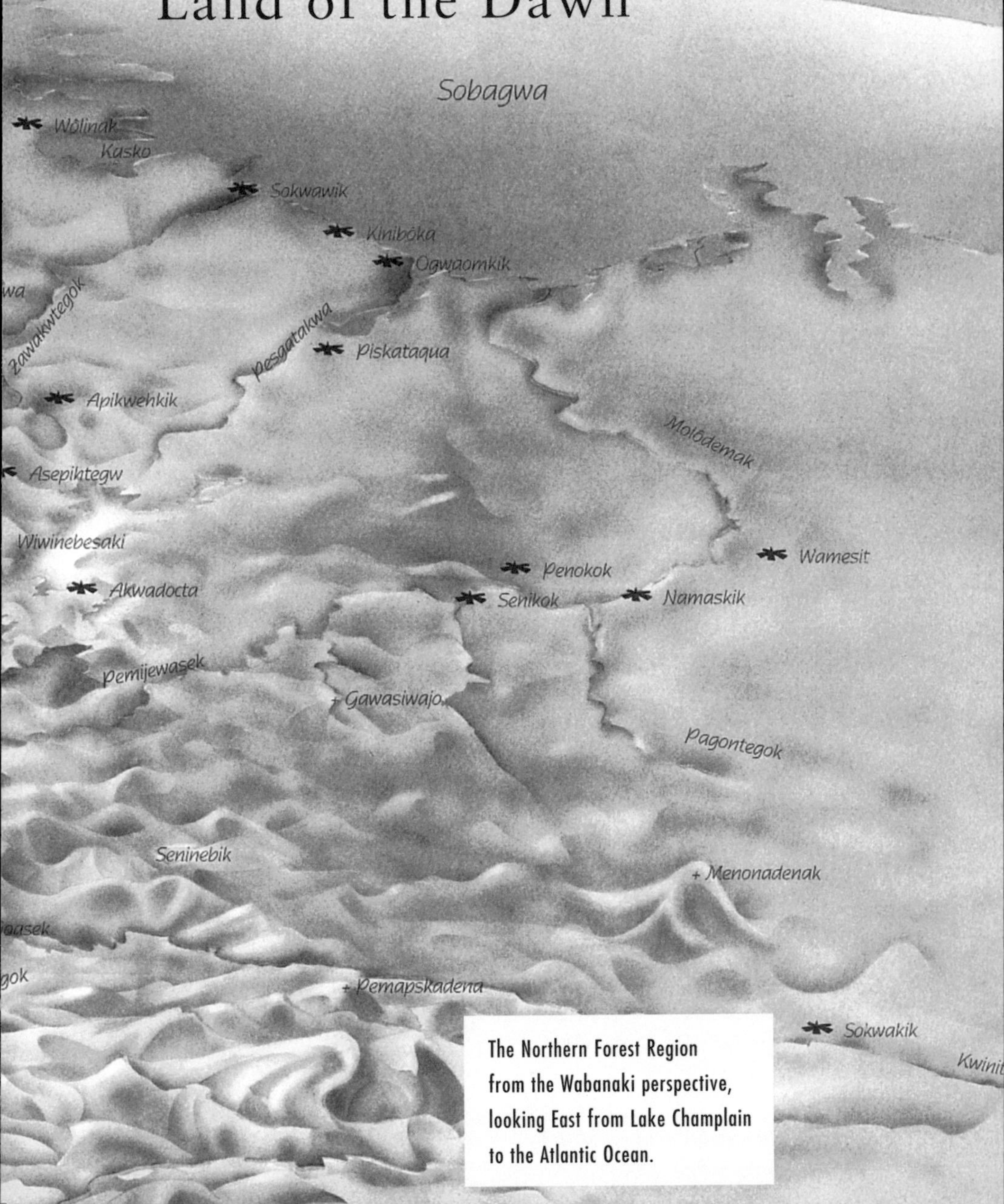

The Northern Forest Region from the Wabanaki perspective, looking East from Lake Champlain to the Atlantic Ocean.

"The French explorers Cartier and Champlain were fortunate enough to stumble across the St. Lawrence River that, more than any other on the East Coast, led deep into the interior...the French adapted centuries-old Native American trade routes and millennia-old canoe designs."

– Willem Lange
Valley News,
March 21, 2003

NEWCOMERS: CONFLICT & CHANGE

As early as 1497, Europeans began exploring along the coast and up the larger rivers of the Northern Forest region. In 1535, French explorer Jacques Cartier reported seeing two bark canoes carrying 17 men. In 1603, Samuel de Champlain described Native American bark canoes between 20 and 23 feet long and 40 to 50 inches wide, capable of carrying about a half ton of cargo, but light enough to be carried by one man. He went on to express admiration for the vessel's speed, reporting that a canoe with just two paddlers could easily pass a fully manned longboat with four oarsmen.

From the Native Americans, European arrivals learned that the canoe was the most efficient means of exploring and traveling through the Northern Forest's interior wilds—but not before their presence led to devastating changes for tribal communities. Introduced diseases spread quickly through Native American populations. European demand for furs disrupted traditional hunting patterns by creating incentives for over-trapping of beaver and other fur-bearing mammals.

Gifts and Curses

The arrival of Europeans proved a time of gifts and a time of curses. Trade goods such as kettles, axes, muskets, and blankets eased daily life for most Native American peoples. But other introductions were not as welcome. Epidemics of smallpox and measles swept through Native American communities, killing thousands. European settlements and land feuds interrupted traditional patterns of hunting, gathering, and growing food, leading to the breakdown of family and tribal relationships. From an estimated population of 40,000 prior to European arrival, disease and war left fewer than 1,000 Abenaki after the American Revolution.

As these animals became scarce along major waterways, trappers used canoes to travel up smaller streams and into headwater regions in search of pelts to trade—eventually trapping beaver nearly to extinction. Many Native American people followed water routes north into what is now Québec—seeking refuge from the disease and disruption ravaging communities along the coast and major river systems.

Europeans in the 1600s proved only occasional visitors to the Northern Forest region; two centuries later, they were permanent residents. As their interest in the new land grew, so did competition for control of its vast resources, first between Europeans and Native American peoples, later primarily between the French and the English. Each of the colonial powers treated and used Native American lands differently. The French expressed interest in land, resources, and trade, with a particular interest in valuable beaver pelts. The English, on the other hand, proved land hungry, and came to North America in farming families.

Each of the colonial powers treated and used Native American lands differently.

The Northern Forest and surrounding lands soon became the setting for a series of wars between European powers for control of the North American continent, with the canoe trails defining important routes that often meant the difference between victory and defeat. For almost 100 years, the French and Indian Wars followed the rivers, shifting back-and-forth from north to south and east to west in a series of seemingly unending raids, counter-raids, and changes of alliance.

Attack and Escape along the Lakes and Rivers

While Northern Forest lakes and rivers served as avenues for peaceful trade and travel, these waterways also played critical roles in military strategy. In this context, they became the attack roads, the escape routes, and sometimes the downfall of a campaign.

A particularly horrific example is that of Rogers' Raid. In 1759, Robert Rogers and his New Hampshire Rangers attacked the French-allied Abenaki village of St. Francis near Montreal. On Lake Champlain, they hid by day and rowed north by night to Missisquoi Bay. From there, they force-marched through bog and forest with a squad of French and Abenaki warriors in pursuit, to attack and decimate the unsuspecting village. Pursued by the Abenaki, Rogers' Rangers took a little-known escape route south, past Lake Memphremagog and along the Clyde and Nulhegan Rivers. Victory Bog holds two graves believed to contain the remains of Rangers who died on the retreat; many more allegedly died or deserted along the way. The ragged, starving soldiers stumbled into the Coos Intervales, Abenaki farm fields along the Connecticut River. Near the mouth of the Upper Ammonoosuc River, most could go no farther. Rogers built a crude raft and, with a couple of his men, drifted down the Connecticut River to safety at British Fort #4.

Pursued by the Abenaki, Rogers' Rangers took a little-known escape route south, past Lake Memphremagog and along the Clyde and Nulhegan Rivers.

Two decades later, during the American Revolution, Colonel Benedict Arnold, aided by Abenaki guides including the Abenaki leader Sabatis, mounted an attack to take Québec and the St. Lawrence River from the British. He led 1,100 soldiers to Fort Western in Augusta and commissioned the quick building of 200 river-boats, or bateaux. Each flat-bottomed boat measured between 25 and 30 feet, weighed nearly 400 pounds waterlogged, and had been shoddily constructed of green wood. "We traveled," Arnold wrote, "up the wild Kennebec River, then through an entangled wilderness on the Dead River, a bruising, flesh-tearing portage-march while the food and supplies gave out." By the time Arnold reached Canada, all of the bateaux had sunk or been smashed in rapids, and half of his men had deserted. Forty Native American canoes were procured for the attack, but the remaining men, starving and injured, were quickly defeated.

Lake Champlain, Water Route Extraordinaire

If rivers proved primary travel paths, then Lake Champlain was the route extraordinaire. In the Northern Forest region, north led to the St. Lawrence River and ultimately west to the Great Lakes. South led to the Hudson River and on to the Atlantic Ocean. As a result, Lake Champlain remained enormously important militarily.

History has witnessed more Euro-American conflicts on the Lake than on any other inland water body in North America. Samuel de Champlain brought firearms to the Lake in his 1609 effort to assist a group of eastern Native American people against their Iroquois enemies. During the 1776 Battle of Valcour Island, the British sunk Benedict Arnold's gondola, the Philadelphia, which was salvaged from the lake bottom 159 years later. The Americans had their turn in 1814, when Captain MacDonough's ingenuity led to the defeat of the superior British fleet in Plattsburgh Bay, ending a campaign to cleave the United States in half via Lake Champlain.

"The Connecticut River Lumber Company's gang of river men have commenced operations on their lumber. They will drive 80,000,000 feet of lumber down the Connecticut River this season. Which is greatly in excess of the quantity heretofore driven down the river. The company employs 1,000 men, and at present prices, the expenses of driving will exceed $3,000 per day. It will, with a good pitch of water, take from 90 to 100 days to put the lumber into their booms at Holyoke, Mass., and Hartford, Conn., where it is to be delivered."

– *The Northern Sentinel,*
April 29, 1881

RIVERS FOR SETTLEMENT & INDUSTRY

The American Revolution's end found Euro-Americans living mostly in villages and towns clustered along the Atlantic seacoast, with thin lines of population following the river valleys into the interior lands. They sought the vast areas of land lying to the north and west of the settled seacoast, and many eagerly set about the task of changing this land to fit their vision of an expanding nation. Gradually, pioneer families moved inland in search of land on which to build homes and farms, and often rivers and water trails led them to their new homesteads. Settlement by Euro-American families in remote areas along what is now the Northern Forest Canoe Trail typically involved the men of a family traveling by canoe into the forest to find a suitable location, clearing a lot, and building a cabin. This work could take up to five summers, with the men returning downriver to town for the winter months. Come spring, they would

Fragments of Saranac History

The Saranac River illustrates the interplay of water and industry through history. A paddle down this valley reveals a progression from wilderness to rural farms to town and industry, and sometimes, back to rural. The remains of the grand schemes and powerful industries that once drank from the river are visible in the broken stone of bridge abutments and scattered beams, and of dams piled along the shore. The river flows past a carry trail by sites of former industries: a shingle mill, a tannery, a glass works, a factory and canal, sawmills, pulp mills and the Saranac Iron Works. Red stones at a traditional Saranac River ford identify the site of the 19th century Redford "Crown Glass" factory which supported fine homes for its owners, as shown above. These dams and historic sites are really a tally of puzzle pieces, that, when fitted together, give us a picture of the Saranac as a very different river than the one we now see burbling, almost forgotten, through the city of Plattsburgh, in eastern New York.

retrace their steps into the woods, eventually bringing wives, children, and supplies to set up subsistence farms and new lives.

As one local historian noted, the challenge Europeans faced settling these northern lands sometimes proved so difficult that "the first efforts to settle the Fulton Chain region [New York] ended soon after 1803, when one discouraged settler after another wearily headed south leaving a few clearings to the wolves and the brambles." It was clear in these early years that the immediate and pressing need was for improved transportation systems such as all-weather roads, snag-free rivers, canals, and, eventually, railroads to link isolated communities.

Moving into forests that had sustained Native American peoples for thousands of years, settlers cleared timber, tilled land, and established farms.

Such changes did not come quickly to the Northern Forest. The nearness of an unprotected Canadian border, and the fevers that still swept through the land, kept most people away. Easier settlement could be found to the south, along the major river trails and already-defended portages. Gradually, though, settlements grew and pushed inland along established canoe routes. Moving into forests that had sustained Native American peoples for thousands of years, settlers cleared timber, tilled land, and established farms.

Trade and communication during this period increased along the waterways of the Northern Forest, facilitated in large part by the canoes, snowshoes, toboggans and baskets made by Native American peoples. Merchants and farmers transported farm goods downstream for trading in larger cities and towns, and city-made goods traveled back upstream. As more people set up farmsteads along rivers like the Saranac and Missisquoi, interest grew in harnessing waterpower to grind corn and process other crops produced in the new settlements. Mills soon sprang up along the rivers. First, gristmills were built, followed by sawmills and turning mills, and eventually modern pulp and paper mills to process the region's abundant timber.

Harvesting and transporting timber to downstream mills and markets led to perhaps the most legendary and celebrated uses of the waters of the Northern Forest Canoe Trail: the river drives.

During the 19th century, great spruce trees in the Northern Forest provided lumber to build the growing cities of the eastern United States. Early in the 20th century, as the old-growth spruce and pine became scarce, demand shifted to mid-sized spruce and fir trees to feed the growing pulp and paper industry. Harvesting and transporting timber to downstream mills and markets led to perhaps the most legendary and celebrated uses of the waters of the Northern Forest Canoe Trail: the river drives.

Timber companies such as New Hampshire's Brown Company, which eventually owned acreage equal to the size of Rhode Island,

The Lake That Was Once Two Towns

Flagstaff Lake rests in a scenic valley beside Maine's Bigelow Mountain range, but its history is quite different from similar lakes. As one nearby resident observes, "There are still paved roads under that lake." That's because the lake is actually man-made, created as a hydropower reservoir in 1949 by Central Maine Power Company. The power company bought out residents, moved buildings or simply razed them, and even relocated the dearly departed from their resting sites to new cemeteries, before clear-cutting everything in the basin below the 1,144-foot contour line and raising the water level of the Dead River.

"Paddle the shallow waters of Flagstaff Lake today," wrote Edgar Allen Beem in *Down East* magazine, "and you are floating above the sunken remains of the homes and businesses, fields and farms, forest lands and family histories that residents of Flagstaff and Dead River were forced to sacrifice fifty years ago to the greater good of electrical power."

bought land not so much for the quality of its timber, but for its proximity to rivers (in this case, the Androscoggin). Each fall, lumbermen left their farms to spend the winter in logging camps deep in the woods—cutting trees and piling them along the banks of rivers and lakes. When the ice went out, the river drivers floated the logs downstream with the spring freshet, sometimes riding the rafts of logs, sometimes wading into frigid water to push the logs along, sometimes risking their lives to break logjams in raging rapids. These became the legendary north woods log drives.

As happened elsewhere in the Northeast, railroads and trucks, which could get logs to the markets much more quickly, eventually made the great river drives a memory.

The remoteness of the north woods presented river drivers with communication problems that required creativity to solve. Each spring, check dams on the North, Yellow, Black, and East Branches of Vermont's Nulhegan River held water back to flood the streams enough to float the logs. But the drives on each tributary had to be carefully timed to follow one another, otherwise the logs would all meet each other at the confluence with the Connecticut River in one enormous and disastrous stickpile. How could this be done from four different stream valleys? Lumbermen built a series of semaphore towers on hilltops and signaled when to open each check dam and send logs tumbling down to the Connecticut River. The last Nulhegan log drive occurred in the 1940s. As happened elsewhere in the Northeast, railroads and trucks, which could get logs to the markets much more quickly, eventually made the great river drives a memory.

Smugglers' Cave

During the Prohibition period (1920 to 1933), "rumrunners" smuggling Canadian liquor along back roads into the United States took to the water to avoid increasingly persistent lawmen. Lake Champlain and Lake Memphremagog, straddling the international border, served as major bootlegging routes, conveying everything from a few bottles stashed in a rowboat to entire barges filled with barrels of Canadian whiskey.

On Lake Memphremagog, under the shoulder of Owl's Head Mountain, Smugglers' Cave hid illegal contraband, stashed until the moonless nights that allowed for runners to elude patrolmen. "The bottom is rumored to hold many bottles of booze, a few liquor-laden boats, more than one body, and a handful of cars that failed to complete the trip down the lake," wrote Scott Wheeler, in *Rumrunners and Revenuers: Prohibition in Vermont.*

"The poet must, from time to time, travel the logger's path and the Indian's trail, to drink at some new and more bracing fountain of the Muses, far in the recesses of the wilderness."

– Henry David Thoreau
The Maine Woods
1864

RECREATION, RENEWAL & CONSERVATION

Just as many people valued the Northern Forest for its abundant natural resources and wealth, others saw the region as a perfect antidote to the pressures and pollution of America's growing cities.

Artists and philosophers like Frederick Church, Ralph Waldo Emerson, and Henry David Thoreau saw nature as a place to reconnect with the spirit of God, and they saw the Northern Forest as a place to experience nature in its true, wild state. While traveling in Maine's Moosehead Lake and Allagash regions in 1857, Thoreau noted, "It is wonderful how well watered this country is... Generally, you may go in any direction in a canoe, by making frequent but not very long portages."

Not long after the Civil War's end, many who had lived through the conflagration grew concerned about what they saw as a growing national lethargy. Writers of the time suggested that this could be cured through the application of a more vigorous living shaped by contact with wilderness. "I wish to preach, not the doctrine of ignoble ease, but the doctrine of the strenuous life, the life of toil and effort, of labor and strife," observed Vice President Theodore

Roosevelt in 1899. "To preach that highest form of success which comes, not to the man who desires mere easy peace, but to the man who does not shrink from danger, from hardship, or from bitter toil, and who out of these wins the splendid ultimate triumph." At the same time, the growing congestion of eastern cities led many people to follow the lead of artists and philosophers and seek retreat, health, and renewal in the wilds of the Northern Forest.

As young men from Boston, New York, and Philadelphia sought to prove their "soldier's faith" by facing the mountains and rivers of the Northern Forest, canoeing became a popular sport. By 1900, canoe clubs flourished around the country, especially in the northeast.

The Healing Waters

During the mid-1800s, 31 lavish spas, modeled after their loftier European counterparts, sprang up in Vermont, built by enterprising business people that tapped into the area's 126 mineral springs. Well-to-do visitors came north to seek health in these beautiful settings, and enjoyed doing so in the company of their social peers. Disease during that time remained largely uncontrollable. Thus, an establishment such as Sheldon's Missisquoi Springs Hotel became a popular destination, fueled by the rumors of the waters' curative powers for the likes of cancer and consumption. Brunswick Springs and Highgate were well known from the times of early Native American people; the Abenaki called the place *nebizonnebik*, or "at the medicine water." Brunswick Springs is still considered a sacred spot with natural healing powers.

Indeed, the image of the canoe was so powerful that it even invaded the western culture of "cowboy and Indian," with popular "dime novels" often portraying Native Americans of the plains in the unlikely activity of sluicing along rapids in birch-bark canoes.

Over time, recreation emerged as a major economic force along many parts of the Northern Forest Canoe Trail, as more and more people came to hunt, fish, relax, and explore the vast northern waterways and wilderness. In some areas, sporting camps catering to hunting and fishing enthusiasts sprouted along rivers and lakes deep in the forest—often accessible only by boat. In other places, grand resorts and hotels invited wealthy visitors seeking to combine wilderness and luxury experiences. As travel routes from the south improved, more people were able to escape the cities to vacation in communities like Rangeley, Maine and Raquette Lake, New York.

Canoe and boat builders flourished and developed customized craft to match the character of local waterways and the interests of visitors.

Canoe and boat builders flourished and developed customized craft to match the character of local waterways and the interests of visitors. Penobscot craftsmen pioneered the creation of the wood-canvas canoe as well as modern paddle types. The Adirondack guideboat and the Rangeley boat were both designed primarily for use by guides transporting their clients (or "sports" as they were called) on fishing trips on lakes and broad rivers. Local Native Americans became the most important guides in Maine, Vermont, and the Adirondacks, and Native American women made many of the baskets and tourist novelties that became an important part of the myth of the New England wilderness. Gradually people came to view the systems of rivers and lakes not as a series of vital travel and trade routes, but rather as individual venues for recreational fishing and camping trips.

"Flyrod" Crosby

Pioneer sportswoman Cornelia Crosby is famed as Maine's first registered guide. During the 1890s, she had the reputation for catching more fish than any other Maine woman, and this with a fly rod. This was quite a turnaround for a woman who took to the outdoors only because she had tuberculosis and was anemic and sickly. Following doctors' orders, she returned to her home in Phillips and learned to hunt and fish—eventually becoming a guide, working out of the posh Rangeley hotels, and competing with male guides for the wealthy clients. She was one of Maine's first outdoor writers, and became a hit at sportsmen's shows, conducting fly tying and casting demonstrations in what was then a "brave" outfit—her skirt ended a full seven inches from the floor. "Flyrod" Crosby—who lived to be 93 years old—paved the way for many women and men after her who love the outdoors and the rivers.

Recreation proved only a beginning, though, for many involved in rediscovering the Northern Forest. As residents and visitors alike paddled the rivers and lakes of the ancient canoe trails, they began to recognize the impact of years of conflict, trapping, agriculture, forestry, and industry. In 1880, the American Canoe Association was chartered with a stated public mission of conservation. Other organizations quickly followed—including the Society for the Protection of New Hampshire Forests and the Appalachian Mountain Club. The New York Legislature passed a bill establishing the Adirondack Park in 1892, strengthened two years later through a state constitutional amendment. The Park includes long stretches of the western Northern Forest Canoe Trail. In 1970, the Allagash Wilderness Waterway became the first designated state-administered wild river in the National Wild and Scenic Rivers System. The impact of these northern river resources was so strong that native Westerner, Supreme Court Justice, and ardent conservationist William O. Douglas once said of the Allagash River's sinuous stretches: "There are no hundred miles in America quite their equal."

Recreation proved only a beginning, though, for many involved in rediscovering the Northern Forest.

The work of scores of environmental organizations has led to continued conservation of the Northern Forest. During the past few years, large landowners who controlled much of the Northern Forest have negotiated to conserve hundreds of thousands of acres of forestland, much of it along the canoe trail, in partnership with public agencies and private conservation groups.

The Northern Forest Canoe Trail benefits from the legacy of these conservation initiatives, as it passes through more than 35 extraordinary national and state wildlife refuges, conservation areas, and parks.

"The history of humankind…has been tied closely to the rivers…Times, however, have changed greatly in some respects, and our lives are no longer bound so intimately to the flowing waters. But for many people the rivers are no less important today than they ever were—if only for the spiritual gifts they carry."

– Charles W. Johnson,
The Nature of Vermont
1998

THE NORTHERN FOREST CANOE TRAIL TODAY

The Northern Forest Canoe Trail serves as a thread, weaving together the historical, cultural, and natural character of this unique Northern Forest region. Travelers exploring the region today by car or by boat find people who still make traditional wood-canvas canoes. They find wilderness guides, sporting camps, anglers, and sportsmen. They encounter visitors and locals alike exploring the region's waterways as a means of experiencing and connecting with the natural world. They experience communities that once turned their backs to the rivers and now value and invest in their waterfronts. As travelers on the Northern Forest Canoe Trail paddle past beaver ponds, meandering streams, whitewater rapids, cities, towns, and wide lakes, they also pass through a human history of subsistence, exploration, settlement, conflict, industry, recreation, and conservation.

In earlier days, small boats were the only way to penetrate the vast Northern Forest woods. Human-powered craft like canoes and kayaks continue to be the best way to explore the Northern Forest Canoe Trail. To complete the entire 740-mile trail, paddlers need to muster all their paddling skills—to line or pole upstream, descend Class IV rapids, cross large, exposed lakes subject to wind and waves, and to portage—the same challenges faced by navigators throughout history. In 2000, Donnie Mullen became the first person in modern history to canoe the entire route. The odyssey took him 50 days in a wood and canvas 16-foot canoe that he built himself. "Canoeing is my preferred mode of wilderness travel and I love to be outside," he says. "The trip was an adventure, and it's amazing to realize that it is still possible to cross the northeast by canoe."

In Fort Kent, the old blockhouse bears witness to the long conflict for control of the region's natural resources.

The names of rivers like the Missisquoi and Ammonoosuc remind us of the first peoples to live and explore along this ancient route, and who continue to live along and travel these waters. In Fort Kent, the old blockhouse bears witness to the long conflict for control of the region's natural resources. Granite pylons along the Connecticut River reveal deserted railroad lines that once helped open the Northern Forest to commerce. All that remains of the lost towns of Dead River and Flagstaff are the memories kept in the local historical society in Stratton, Maine. In the Vermont town of Brighton, the Nulhegan River slips quietly past Mill Street—only a name left to tell us where the sawmill once stood. At the far western end of the trail, paddlers share the route with the Fulton Chain steamers *Clearwater* and *Uncas* or watch the *President Harrison* slide by as it travels the longest freshwater mail run in the United States.

Despite the changes they have witnessed, the water trails are here for us still—to learn from, to care for, to use, and to enjoy. Look closely and you will see the passage of time, the depth of human history, and the power of water to move us in so many remarkable ways.

Flora and Fauna of the Northern Forest

The Northern Forest Canoe Trail's watersheds host a range of birds, mammals, and plants. Moose sightings are common; the call of the loon brings magic to the northern night; the smallest creature or flower delights; and a great blue heron just may lead you around the next bend.

AFTERWORD

The travel routes of the Abenaki, and the many kinds of bark and dugout canoes for all types of water, live on today despite all of the dramatic changes in the Northern Forest region. These canoe trails are part of an ancient way of life that has quietly survived, often ignored, yet never forgotten. Fort #4 in Charlestown, New Hampshire, houses an early 20th century birch bark canoe made in the old Abenaki way by Robert Paquette at Odanak. Simosis Obomsawin made birch bark canoes from scratch at Thompson's Point in Charlotte, Vermont in the mid-20th century. Young Abenaki canoe and dugout makers like Aaron York and James Bruchac carry on old skills in their workshops today.

Most remarkably, even in the 19th and 20th centuries, the old ways of travel continued. One account of Abenaki birch bark canoes in action describes a trip from Lake Champlain to Philadelphia by canoe via Lake George and the Hudson, Raritan, Delaware, and Schuylkill Rivers to trade hand-made baskets and other crafts. Another account speaks of an Abenaki family traveling up the St. Francis River in Québec, and down the Connecticut, with all of their belongings. A third describes a family canoe trip from Missisquoi to Hanover, New Hampshire via Lake Champlain and the Connecticut River. Just remember, when you come to portages with grandmother, she stays in the canoe!

After the much-storied 17th and 18th century heyday of the birch bark canoe and the Indian wars, most of us forgot our rivers, and that older way of life. Yet, indigenous ways of life still endure. Now, people of all ages have become interested in Native American ways of life. As time has gone on, the Abenaki campsite ethic—always leave a campsite clean and stocked with plenty of dry wood, a source of fire, and a clear way to good water—has become a way of life for many in the Northern Forest. The Abenaki have always protected the good campsites, and the many sacred and traditional places along the rivers, to honor the ancient past of their ancestors, and to respect this good land, and the waters, and all life for seven generations to come.

As time has gone on, the Abenaki campsite ethic—always leave a campsite clean and stocked with plenty of dry wood, a source of fire, and a clear way to good water—has become a way of life for many in the Northern Forest.

– John Moody
The Winter Center for Indigenous Traditions

THE NORTHERN FOREST CANOE TRAIL ORGANIZATION

Incorporated in 2000, the Northern Forest Canoe Trail is a non-profit, membership organization whose mission is *to celebrate the rich human heritage and diverse natural environment of the Northern Forest by establishing and stewarding a water trail tracing historic Native American travel routes across New York, Vermont, Québec, New Hampshire, and Maine.*

The idea for the Trail was brought to life in the 1990's when Mike Krepner, Ron Canter, and Randy Mardres of Native Trails, Inc. researched the traditional east-west water routes used by Native Americans and early settlers in the Northern Forest region. Kay Henry and Rob Center, former management principals of the Mad River Canoe Company, formed the Northern Forest Canoe Trail organization as a way to translate this research into a recreational, community, and regional resource. From the outset, the Northern Forest Canoe Trail has distinguished itself as a can-do, action-oriented non-profit, committed to making the Trail accessible for recreation, expressive of regional culture and heritage, and meaningful in very concrete ways to the local communities through which it passes.

The Northern Forest Canoe Trail organization delivers its mission through three program areas that our small but resourceful staff coordinates with more than 200 volunteers along the length of the Trail:

1) *Waterway Stewardship:* In collaboration with local partners, we initiate and support a range of on-the-ground projects that promote healthy, accessible waterways and riparian areas, and that foster greater connections between residents and their watersheds.

2) *Rural Economic Development:* The Trail is a celebration of both people and place, and in that spirit, the Northern Forest Canoe Trail organization is committed to positioning the Trail to benefit local communities. Our primary focus in this arena is on promoting sustainable or nature-based tourism whose benefits accrue at the local level in terms of new opportunities for small businesses and services.

3) *Recreation, Arts, and Heritage:* The waterways of the Northern Forest Canoe Trail are brimming with stories about the rich history of the human and natural communities of the Northern Forest region. We are committed to supporting community-based efforts to share and celebrate these stories through events, arts projects, and educational programs.

For more information, or to become involved, please contact:

NORTHERN FOREST CANOE TRAIL
P.O. Box 565, Waitsfield, Vermont 05673
802.496.2285 (tel); 802.496.2785 (fax)
email: info@NorthernForestCanoeTrail.org
www.NorthernForestCanoeTrail.org

"Most of the time, the only sounds were the repeated splash of our paddles, the whisper of a gentle breeze, and our occasional exclamations about the beauty of the surroundings."

– Victor Block
Maine Sunday Telegram
October 2, 2005

RESOURCES, NOTES & ARTWORK CREDITS

RESOURCES

MUSEUMS & HISTORICAL ASSOCIATIONS

New York

The Adirondack Museum
State Route 30, P.O. Box 99
Blue Mountain Lake, NY 12812
518-352-7311
www.adirondackmuseum.org

Adirondack Park Visitor Interpretive Centers
State Route 30, P.O. Box 3000
Paul Smiths, NY 12970, 518-327-3000
State Route 28N, P.O. Box 101
Newcomb, NY 12852, 518-582-2000
www.adkvic.org

Akwesasne Cultural Center
321 State Route 37
Hogansburg, NY 13655
518-358-2240
www.nc3r.org/akwlibr

Battle of Plattsburgh Interpretive Center
31 Washington Road
Plattsburgh, NY 12901
518-566-1814
www.battleofplattsburgh.org

Clinton County Historical Association
3 Cumberland Avenue
Plattsburgh, NY 12901
518-561-0340
www.clintoncountyhistorical.org

Great Camp Sagamore
State Route 28, P.O. Box 40
Raquette Lake, NY 13436
315-354-5311
www.sagamore.org

Natural History Museum of the Adirondacks
45 Museum Drive
Tupper Lake, NY 12986
518-359-7800
www.wildcenter.org

Saranac Lake Free Library
109 Main Street
Saranac Lake, NY 12983
518-891-4190
www.nnyln.net/slfl/index.htm

Six Nations Indian Museum
Franklin County Road 30, HCR 1 Box 10
Onchiota, NY 12989
518-891-2299
http://tuscaroras.com/graydeer/pages/sixnamus.htm

Town of Webb Historical Association
State Route 28, P.O. Box 513
Old Forge, NY 13420
315-369-3838
www.webbhistory.org

Vermont

Abenaki Tribal Museum
100 Grand Avenue
Swanton, VT 05488
802-868-2559
www.abenakination.org/museums.html

ECHO at the Leahy Center for Lake Champlain
One College Street
Burlington, VT 05401
802-864-1848
www.echovermont.org

Fairbanks Museum and Planetarium
1302 Main Street
St. Johnsbury, VT 05819
802-748-2372
www.fairbanksmuseum.org

Lake Champlain Maritime Museum
4472 Basin Harbor Road
Vergennes, VT 05491
802-475-2022
www.lcmm.org

Memphremagog Historical Society Museum
Emory Hebard State Office Building
200 Main Street
Newport, VT 05855
802-334-2813

Swanton Railroad Depot Museum
58 South River Street
Swanton, VT 05488
802-868-5436
www.swantonhistoricalsociety.org

Vermont Folklife Center
3 Court Street
Middlebury, VT 05753
802-388-4964
www.vermontfolklifecenter.org

Vermont Historical Society
109 State Street, Pavilion Building
Montpelier, VT 05609
802-828-2291
www.vermonthistory.org

New Hampshire

New Hampshire Historical Society/ Museum of New Hampshire History
6 Eagle Square
Concord, NH 03301
603-228-6688
www.nhhistory.org

Northern Forest Heritage Park
961 Main Street
Berlin, NH 03570
603-752-7202
www.northernforestheritage.org

Stark Museum
224 Denmark Street
Berlin, NH 03582
603-752-3265

Maine

Acadian Archives / Archives acadiennes
University of Maine at Fort Kent
23 University Avenue
Fort Kent, ME 04743
207-834-7535
www.umfk.maine.edu/archives

Dead River Area Historical Society
Route 27
Stratton, ME 04982
Open Memorial Day through Labor Day
207-246-2271
www.mainemuseums.org

Fort Kent State Historic Site
Off Route 1
Fort Kent, ME 04743
207-941-4014
Open Memorial Day through Labor Day
www.state.me.us/cgi-bin/doc/parks/find_one_name.pl?park_id=56

Maine Historical Society
485 Congress Street
Portland, ME 04101
207-774-1822
www.mainehistory.com

Maine Folklife Center
University of Maine
5773 South Stevens Hall, Room 112B
Orono, ME 04469
www.umaine.edu/folklife

Maine State Museum
83 State House Station
Augusta, ME 04333
207-287-2301
www.state.me.us/museum

Moosehead Historical Society
444 Pritham Avenue, P.O. Box 1116
Greenville, ME 04441
207-695-2909
www.mooseheadhistory.org

Moosehead Marine Museum
12 Lily Bay Road, P.O. Box 1151
Greenville, ME 04441
207-695-2716
www.katahdincruises.com/museum.html

Penobscot Nation Museum
5 Center Street,
Indian Island, ME 04468
207-827-4153
www.penobscotnation.org/museum/
index.htm

Rangeley Lakes Region
Logging Museum
Route 16, P.O. Box 154
Rangeley, ME 04970
207-864-3939

NOTES

PREFACE

(page 8) Quotation: Ron Canter, Adirondack Life, 2002 Annual Guide, p.65

THE STORY OF THE NORTHERN FOREST CANOE TRAIL

(page 14) Quotation: Stephen Gorman, Northeastern Wilds: Journeys of Discovery in the Northern Forest (Appalachian Mountain Club, 2002), p. 23

WATERWAYS & THE FIRST PEOPLES

(page 18) Quotation: David Cook, Above the Gravel Bar: The Indian Canoe Routes of Maine (Milo Printing Company, 1985), p. 39

(page 19) "Into this new land...": Maine Archaeological Society web page, state.me.us/mhpc/archaeol.htm

(page 19) "Trade between tribes...": Patrick Jennings, (National Park Service, Boston: unpublished research paper, 2002)

(page 20) "East-west travel proved difficult...": Gordon Day, In Search of New England's Native American Past (Foster & Cowan, 1998)

Sidebar: Ice One Mile Thick
(page 21) "Between 35,00 and 15,000 years ago...":
Patrick Jennings, (National Park Service, Boston: unpublished research paper, 2002) and Michael Waters, Principles of American Geoarchaeology: A North American Perspective (University of Arizona Press, 1993)

Sidebar: Small Boat
(page 22) Quotation: Edwin Tappan Adney and Howard I. Chapelle, The Bark Canoes and Skin Boats of North America (The Smithsonian Institution, 1964), p. 13

(page 23) "A typical 15-foot birchbark canoe..." and "The Penobscot Indians called...": Tux Turkel, Glacial Melt, Birch Bark Gave People Means to Travel, (www.outdoors.mainetoday.com/forgotten/glacier.htm, 1997)

(page 23) "One person could...": Nature Bulletin No. 463-A, Forest Preserve District of Cook County, (www.newton.dep.anl.gov/natbltn/400-499/nb463.htm)

(page 23) Father Rasle quotation, Father Rasle's letter to his brother dated Oct 12, 1723: M. Calvert, Dawn Over the Kennebec (Mary Calvert Books, 1984) pp. 108-111;

Sidebar: Abenaki Village Sites
(page 24) Nicholas Muller and Samuel Hand, In a State of Nature: Readings in Vermont History (VT Historical Society, 1982) pp. 22-23

NEWCOMERS: CONFLICT & CHANGE

(page 28) Quotation: Willem Lange, "My Appreciation for Canoes Now Has an Historical Dimension", (A Yankee Notebook column, Valley News, Lebanon, NH, 3/21/03)

(page 29) "As early as 1497...": Edwin Tappan Adney and Howard I. Chapelle, The Bark Canoes and Skin Boats of North America (The Smithsonian Institution, 1964)

Sidebar: Gifts and Curses
(page 30) European diseases and population estimates: First Nations Histories (www.tolatsga.org/aben.html)

(page 31) Rogers' Rangers story: Ron Canter, Past and Present in the Northeast Kingdom of Vermont, (unpublished paper, June 2001)

(page 32) Benedict Arnold story: Frank Lewis, "Arnold Invades Québec", (Wooden Canoe Journal Issue #73, Feb 1996, www.WCHA.org)

(page 32) "We traveled..." Quotation from Benedict Arnold, Flowing Past: Maine's Kennebec and Dead Rivers; (Maine PBS documentary)

Sidebar: Lake Champlain, Water Route Extraordinaire
(page 33) Jan Albers, Hands on the Land (MIT Press, 2000), p. 166

(page 33) "...more Euro-American conflicts on the Lake...": Around the Lake — A Guide to Historic Sites on Lake Champlain (UVM Historic Preservation Program, 1996)

(page 33) Captain Thomas Macdonough story: Ron Canter (unpublished paper, June 2003)

RIVERS FOR SETTLEMENT & INDUSTRY

(page 34) Quotation: From Gil Center, History of the Town of Colebrook, NH (1950), p.70

Sidebar: Fragments of Saranac History
(page 36) Ron Canter, Fragments of Saranac History: Union Falls to Plattsurgh (unpublished paper, June 2001)

(page 37) "...first efforts to settle the Fulton Chain...": David H. Beetle, Up Old Forge Way and West Canada Creek (North Country Books, 1984)

(page 37) "Such changes...": Patrick Jennings, (National Park Service, Boston: unpublished research paper, 2002)

(page 38) Brown Company history: Ronald and Grace Jager, New Hampshire: An Illustrated History of the Granite State (Windsor Publications, 1983), p. 224

Sidebar: The Lake That Was Once Two Towns
(page 39) Michele Pavitt, "Flagstaff: Maine's Most Unusual Lake", (Maine Sunday Telegram, 9/24/2000)

(page 39) Edgar Allen Beem, "Flagstaff", (Down East Magazine, August 1999)

Sidebar: Smuggler's Cave
(page 41) Scott Wheeler, Rumrunners and Revenuers: Prohibition in Vermont (New England Press, 2002), p.115-116

RECREATION, RENEWAL & CONSERVATION

(page 42, 43) Quotations "The poet must..." and "It is wonderful how well watered...": Henry David Thoreau, The Maine Woods (1864)

(page 43, 44) "I wish to preach..." quotation from Theodore Roosevelt, The Strenuous Life (1902)

(page 44) "...soldier's faith...": Patrick Jennings, (National Park Service, Boston: unpublished research paper, 2002), referring to late nineteenth century writers such as Oliver Wendell Holmes, Horace Potter (The Philosophy of Courage, 1888) and Edward Bellamy

Sidebar: The Healing Waters
(page 44) Jan Albers, Hands on the Land (MIT Press, 2000), pp 162-3

Sidebar: "Flyrod" Crosby
(page 46) Cal O'Brien, "Famous Maine Women Fly-Tyers", (The Maine Sportsmen, July 1971)

(page 47) Allagash Wilderness Waterway: Dean Bennett (text for NFCT map 13, 2004)

(page 47) William O. Douglas quotation: From "Saving the Allagash River", (Conservation Times, 1998)

THE NORTHERN FOREST CANOE TRAIL TODAY

(page 48) Quotation: Charles Johnson, The Nature of Vermont (University Press of New England, 1998), p. 156

(page 50) Donnie Mullen quotation: (personal communication, 2003)

ARTWORK CREDITS

- Cover: Missisquoi River with Jay Peak in Background, Vermont – Clyde Smith
- Title Page: Allagash, Maine – Dean Bennett
- Contents Page: Connecticut Lakes Fog, New Hampshire – Clyde Smith
- p. 8: Trapping in the Adirondacks - Winslow Homer, engraved by J.P. Davis, © Sterling and Francine Clark Art Institute, Williamstown, Massachusetts
- p. 9: Rowing – Ed Epstein, Courtesy of the artist
- p. 10: Fred Reckards Canoe on Moose River, Maine – Heman Smith, courtesy of Betty Reckards
- p. 12: Reflection on the Clyde River, Vermont – Jayson Benoit
- p. 14: Fall Canoeing, Maine – Rob Center
- pp. 16-17 (counterclockwise): Clyde River Marshes, Vermont – Laurie Sanders / Sunset over Lake Champlain, Vermont – Kay Henry / Island Pond, Vermont – Clyde Smith / Morning Fog on Chamberlain Lake, Maine – Dean Bennett / Umsaskis Lake, Maine – Clyde Smith / Cows on Missisquoi River, Vermont – Clyde Smith / Androscoggin River, New Hampshire – Mike Prescott / Overview Map – www.MapHero.com

- p. 18: Artist Conception of Abenaki Village – Courtesy of Frederick Wiseman
- p. 20: Artist Conception of Abenaki Paddlers – Courtesy of Frederick Wiseman
- p. 21: St. John River Ice, Maine – Marc Michaud
- p. 22: Indigenous People Poling, 1791 – P. Campbell, from Travels in the interior inhabited parts of North America in the years 1791 and 1792, 1793, New Brunswick Museum, St. John, N.B., #LC 917.1 C18
- p. 23: Paddlers on Chamberlain Lake – P. Harry, (RG 76-P.1 Entry 104 – Talcott #1), Records of Boundary and Claims Commissions and Arbitrations, Record Group 76, National Archives and Records Administration, College Park, Maryland
- p. 24: Making Pottery, Maize Nearby – Sketch by Bea Nelson
- p. 25: Long Lake Haze, New York – Mike Prescott
- pp. 26-27: Wobanakik, Land of the Dawn – © Kevin Ruelle and Frederick Wiseman, a production of the Ethan Allen Homestead
- p. 28: Samuel De Champlain – W. Haskell Coffin, 1923, Courtesy of Clinton Community College, Plattsburgh, New York
- p. 30: Exchange of Gifts (Trading) – Bea Nelson
- p. 31: Western Abenaki (Trapping) – Bea Nelson
- p. 32: Rogers' Rangers, Vermont – Courtesy of National Life Insurance Company
- p. 33: Battle of Lake Champlain – Hugh Reinagle, Courtesy of Battle of Plattsburgh Association
- p. 34: Androscoggin River Full of Logs, New Hampshire – Courtesy of Northern Forest Heritage Park
- p. 36: Redford Dwelling House – Courtesy of Clinton County Historical Association
- p. 37: Bloomfield, Vermont, and North Stratford, New Hampshire, 1913 – Courtesy of Special Collections, University of Vermont
- p. 38: Wausau Paper Mill, New Hampshire – Laurie Sanders / Canoes in Penobscot Pulp Drive – Warren Cochrane, Allagash Canoe Trips
- p. 39: The Flooding of Flagstaff, Maine – Courtesy of the Dead River Area Historical Society
- p. 40: Nulhegan Railroad, Vermont – Courtesy of Island Pond Historical Society
- p. 41: Smuggler's Cave on Lake Memphremagog, Vermont / Québec – Dale Wood, from Scott Wheeler, Rum Runners and Revenuers, 2002
- p. 42: A Good Time Coming – Arthur Fitzwilliam Tait, Courtesy of Adirondack Museum
- p. 43: Dancing Fiddler – Ed Epstein, Courtesy of the artist
- p. 44: Pine Crest Lodge, New Hampshire – Courtesy of Bill Schomburg
- p. 45: A Rangeley Landing – Wallace Nutting, Courtesy of www.WallaceNuttingLibrary.com
- p. 46: Flyrod Crosby Studio Portrait – Courtesy of Maine State Museum
- p. 47: Northeast Carry Horsedrawn Shuttle, 1909, Maine – Courtesy of Linda Koski
- p. 48: Canoe and Kayak Approaching – Clyde Smith
- p. 50: Fort Kent Blockhouse, Maine – Jim Deprey
- p. 51: (clockwise) Heron Profile, Maine – Dean Bennett / Furbish's Lousewort, Maine – Maine Natural Areas Program / Loon Greets the Day, New Hampshire – Christine Adams, Errol, New Hampshire, www.christineadamsphotography.com / Moose, New Hampshire – Clyde Smith / Deer Mouse and Mushrooms, Maine – Dean Bennett
- p. 52: Paddlers in Mist on Round Pond, Maine – Dean Bennett
- p. 53: Abenaki Guides and their Clients, Metcalf Island, Lake Champlain, 1910 – Fred W. Wiseman
- p. 54: Connecticut Lakes Paddlers, New Hampshire – Clyde Smith
- p. 56: Take Out on St. John River, Maine – Julie Isbill, RTCA
- Back Cover: NFCT Locator Map – www.MapHero.com